REMEMBERING POPPA

Tom Hancock and 901 West Dubois
Denison Texas

Stories by
David Bucher and John K Bucher Sr.

written by
John K Bucher Sr.

SIDESHOW
MEDIA GROUP
sideshowmediagroup.com

SIDESHOW MEDIA GROUP

Copyright 2021 ©

David Bucher and John K Bucher Sr.

All rights reserved

Dedicated to all of Tom and Neoma Hancock's descendants,

so they will know from where they came...

Special thanks to Jim Sears
for his fine help in researching Denison and Hancock history.

Contents

FOREWORD 1

STORY ONE: The Concrete Porch. 4

STORY TWO: Virgie's Grave. 12

STORY THREE: Geronimo and Frank James. 20

STORY FOUR: The Doctor's Office 29

STORY FIVE: The Mule 37

STORY SIX: James Westbrook and Sweet Potatoes 44

STORY SEVEN: Family Reunions and Searching for
                            The Lost Dog 52

STORY EIGHT: Zephyrinus Salinas 59

STORY NINE: Cotton Mill Days and Honeybees 64

STORY TEN: Murder In Mayberry. 73

THE LAST WORD: Remembering Poppa 82

Foreword

This is not just a story about our grandfather's life. It is a collection of our most vivid memories of him and how he impacted our lives. He has been gone for over fifty years, yet he remains inside our minds, souls, and hearts. Since people's memories can often vary about the same event, David and I found joy in recalling the same stories in perfect unity. Often, we would each have our own memory with added color we recalled but these were never in conflict. This has been a magical experience to reconstruct the past. Thomas Asbury Hancock was not rich, powerful or famous. He was more. He was our Poppa.

I live in California and my three brothers, David, James, and Daniel live in Denison, Texas. During one phone conversation in late summer of 2020, David and I were winding down our spirited opinions of the Great Pandemic, economic meltdowns in our neighborhoods, and political division tearing our country apart. Just before we concluded our call, David insisted on telling me a story about our grandfather he knew I didn't know. We frequently used his example and life stories to make sense of what modern problems we were curious about. After he told me this wonderful story about how T.A. Hancock dealt with segregation in the south in the early 1960's, he said we should write these down and make a record of this amazing man. I was hungry and wanted to eat, so I told him I would think about it. In the days that followed his words would resurface in my brain. I felt there was something there. We talked about what we wanted to tell and started recording these conversations. There would be over ten hours of these memories.

Poppa had nicknames for most people he encountered, especially his children. As far as grandchildren, I only know of David's and mine. His was Nicodemus and mine was Doctor John. In keeping with his spirit, we decided to use these code names for our actual conversations. These tales mostly took place at 901 West Dubois Street in Denison. Denison is located in North Texas along the Red River that borders Oklahoma. It was mainly a railroad town when we were growing up there in the 1950's and 60's. The MKT Rail Line (Katy) employed hundreds of Denison's families that worked on the train itself, or in the downtown administration offices, or across the street at the Depot, or in the many other stations around town where cars and engines were repaired. Denison had several manufacturing plants that kept the economy growing those days. 901 West Dubois lay in the south part of town called The Cotton Mill District, as the city's only Cotton Mill ran at its hub. The Cotton Mill District looked like many other places in the South in the 1950's that made cotton available to the world. It was poor, but back then we really didn't know it. I think it because of Poppa.

He and our grandmother (Nanny) moved there in the early 1950's after a short stay in Pottsboro, a town a few miles away. They had lived their marriage in Oklahoma and started there before it was a state and called Indian Nation. Their house on Dubois honestly wasn't much, but to David and me it was a magical kingdom away from our parents. The simple frame house sat on the corner and was painted white. The steps up to the porch led into a small living room, and then to the kitchen/ dining table. On our left were two small bedrooms and a bath. The back door opened to a back yard and a well, and beyond that was a large garden (or it seemed it was to us). To the left of the big garden was another garden (west garden), an orchard where he had bees that made honey, and a chicken house/yard. Separating the two gardens was a little house (known as The Little House) where Nanny washed clothes and used a hand ringer before hanging them on a clothesline to dry. The Little House shelved Poppa's tools and Nanny's canned warehouse of corn, peas, beans, peaches and apricots. On the west side of the house was a car port, although there usually weren't any cars unless someone came to visit. 901 West Dubois boasted a water cooler in the summer and a gas heater in the winter. Water came from the well, food was harvested from the gardens, honey hives, and chickens, while love was taught to us daily. It was a simple life back then but to us it seemed vastly complex and wonderful.

STORY ONE

The Concrete Porch

It must have been summertime. Great, big, humid, hot hot hot Texas summertime. We went barefoot from June until September and were clad in cut off pants (homemade shorts that had gotten old or wore holes in the knees). Poppa had a problem and had tried to remedy it for quite a while. His rickety, past its prime, front porch had become a headache. The warped boards rose up in places that the caused the front door to longer function. The porch was unsalvageable and needed replacing. He was weary of having to leave through the back door to go and check the mailbox on the street. Poppa asked his sons and son in laws for help. They all promised they would but after a long while, nothing was done.

Now, Poppa was a skilled farmer, none better. He could plan out dozens of vacant acres at a time, plow them, water and fertilize the growing plants, chop the weeds, hoe the furrows as the crops went taller, shoo the predators, and harvest enough to feed his large family, and sell most of it to keep them safe and warm through fierce Oklahoma winters. Poppa was a decent mechanic too. He had kept ancient farm equipment functioning since he was a boy. He could fix lawn mowers and sometimes an automobile. Poppa was adept at many carpenter jobs as he had help build wooden oil well platforms in the early 1900s. Nanny worked just as hard in fields and harvesting. She canned, cooked and prepared all the meals. She raised and fed the livestock and chickens, and actively took place in the slaughter of them as well. However, Poppa evidently knew little about the fine art of working with concrete. In the summer. In the hot Texas heat.

But things like that never stopped him. He got up one fine Texas morning, ate a hearty breakfast with my seven-year-old brother, David (who was a frequent overnight guest as he really didn't cotton to our home much of the time), and decided to build a new porch. He had removed the floor of the porch, so it was open. He tossed rocks and some old junk inside and planned on using the outer walls as forms for the concrete. He had procured some two by fours to use as smoothing boards to finish the drying concrete. It looked simple in his mind. He could use a few spare hands and bang! A new porch.

After breakfast, David was still in the small kitchen with Nanny.

"Nicodemus, come here." Poppa called from the front room, watching the black and white television and casually smoking a Bull Durham hand rolled cigarette. David went promptly to see what he wanted. "Nicodemus, let's order us some concrete."

"Okay, Poppa, whatever you say."

"Then, look up the number in the telephone book." So, young Nicodemus did exactly that. Poppa reached for the black dial telephone that sat on its own tiny table and handed it to David. Poppa held the phone book and placed his brown finger on an entry.

"Now dial that number and tell the man we want some concrete." David told me he really didn't know any better than to do what he said, so he repeated what Poppa had told him to say.

"I need to order some concrete for my Poppa to make a porch." David gave the man Poppa's address as 901 West DuBois, the correct delivery destination. Finally, the concrete man asked him how old he was, and David spat out his age. The man paused and asked if there were any adults around? "My Poppa's right here."

"Could I talk to him?"

"Yeah." And then David handed the phone receiver to Poppa.

"What's going on?" The concrete man asked Poppa. "Whatever the boy said." Poppa replied and handed the phone back to David. "You want some concrete out at 901 West Dubois, right?

"Right. "David answered.

"How much?" Stumped, David looked at Poppa and inquired "Poppa, do we know how much you want?" Poppa thought for a few seconds and said, "Ask him how much it costs?" The concrete man gave David a price for a small batch and then proceeded to pitch him for a few bucks more he could bring a WHOLE BUNCH. Poppa's eyes lit up at the sales pitch and agreed to the bargain of way too much concrete. That, among other factors was the fatal flaw in his grand plan.

Meanwhile, Nanny was in the kitchen listening and decided to make some calls for additional help. My mother soon sent me (age 12) down to assist and when I arrived Uncle Doc had parked his car and was getting out. Poppa was thrilled we were there but seemed very busy as he and David were gathering boards for the project. It wasn't too long after I got there when a huge Denison Concrete truck pulled up and a man got out. Poppa hurried out to greet the man. I recall the talk was rather loud as the engine roared and kept the tub of concrete turning. We all noticed how hot it had become. Now was the time for Texans to rest in some shade on a porch and enjoy some iced tea. But not us. We were about to go to work.

The concrete man backed the truck a little closer to the porch and began to hook together metal segments that when finished created a tube for the concrete to flow. When the tunnel was long enough to reach the porch, the man looked a Poppa and Poppa nodded "YEAH". The motor whined louder, and the sound of water, cement, sand and gravel mixed thoroughly came fast down the open tunnel, across the front yard and splashed hard into the porch area. The wet gray mass was quickly filling the porch forms. The man yelled to Poppa and asked how it looked, and I came to know later in life that meant was it too wet or too dry? Evidently Poppa thought it was just right and told the man to keep it coming. The man poured the porch frames full of drying concrete and actually a little too much as this slick gray mixture looked like frozen gray ice cream in deep waves across the porch. Some of it lapped up the front door by a few inches.

The concrete man was sweating by now and went to check on the level of remaining concrete. He yelled at Poppa there was still more, and he needed to empty the truck. Poppa sprang into action and ran the wheelbarrow out to the truck and suddenly it was full in just one big plop. Poppa told the man to pour some out by the mailbox and after that to pour some on the ground where the dirt driveway and carport stood. After that, the man checked, and the truck still held some concrete. Telling the man to keep it and take it back to the concrete yard never occurred to our dear Poppa. He ran to the back yard and grabbed some metal buckets and one of Nanny's giant wash tubs. These were quickly filled, and the truck was finally empty. The man drove away, and Poppa told us all the get busy now with working the concrete at the porch.

The trouble was that by now the concrete was getting very hard and dry. All of it. The buckets, the wash tubs, the driveway and the mailbox. We were handed two by fours and David and I were on opposite ends of one as Poppa and Uncle Doc worked the other. We sawed and I thought at the time this was great. Minutes went by and the concrete was unmanageable. It resisted our efforts and we sawed harder. It was no use. The concrete barely moved. We pushed on it and seesawed it and watched our sweat fall on it. The concrete had swollen over the top of the frame and stayed there. It was a rocky mess that resembled the surface of the moon with little craters and valleys. The front door was frozen in hard cement. I had not noticed until now, but as the concrete defied our efforts Poppa realized the truth. I don't think I had ever seen him in such a state but now when we, his grandsons looked at him, we saw horror and defeat on his face. He stopped sawing and so did Uncle Doc. David and I had already become winded and stood and gazed at this monument to 901 West DuBois.

One of the many things I learned from this and other events was to accept defeat but to get over it and move on. Poppa saw the cause was lost and made up his mind to leave and let others try and fix it. He decided to go to his bed, turn on the swamp cooler and sleep off this nightmare. He invited his partner in crime, David, to join him but David declined the offer. We surveyed the situation ourselves as he left. The porch was a huge mess with now firmly set concrete wavy and rocky across the top. The forms bulged with the weight of the load and were showing signs of fatigue. The blobs of concrete out by the mailbox and driveway had turned to stone. I went to the back yard and saw the wheelbarrow full of solid concrete and pushed it over. The wheelbarrow fell over and dumped a solid block of concrete in the yard. Nanny's buckets were split by the weight of the mess and so was her giant wash tub. All of it ruined. As the afternoon wore on, Nanny surveyed the damage and waited until the big folks got off work. She made the many calls to arms as supper time was near. Our parents, aunts and uncles arrived with tools, shovels, pickaxes and quickcrete. They ran a chord from inside the house with a large light to illuminate the chore. Nanny turned on the porch light.

The night wore on as Nanny served supper in shifts and the adults hammered and chiseled away the excess concrete. Men and women were laboring against time. I remember how dirty they were but worked in unison. No one complained about Poppa where I could hear them. As the finish came and a smooth porch which allowed the front door to open transpired, some of our aunt's religious relatives showed up for a visit after a long cross-country trip. She was embarrassed to be seen in such a dirty state, but the other adults laughed it off and went home. It was late but it was over.

I didn't see Poppa for a few days but when I did, he never spoke of that day again. He did enjoy sitting on that grand porch and reading the newspaper. Soon we were on to new adventures and we never thought any less of our Poppa. In fact, I think it gave us a lesson to never fear trying to do the difficult or the downright impossible.

STORY TWO

Virgie's Grave

As David and I went about making this book, we knew we had to make lists of the stories we wanted to include. So, we made lists. We quickly found at least ten or more. They stood out like large posts holding up the fence of our memories about the past. Virgie, had she lived, was one of our aunts. We never heard our mother, or her parents, ever mention her until one day things came to a head. Unbeknownst to our young lives, Poppa held a mountain of grief and guilt over something that happened many years ago.

As we recalled the events of the day, David summed it up by saying "That was a terrible day." It was early in the morning we were loaded in our old Rambler station wagon and drove down to pick up Nanny and Poppa. They were dressed, ready and quickly came to get in the car with us. There was a somber mood and a lot of silence as we drove north over the Denison Dam and into Oklahoma. From Durant we headed east. As kids it felt like a very long and tedious drive, even though it only took eighty or ninety minutes. The air inside the Rambler was heavy and we children had no idea why we were making this trip or even to where we were going. A lot has changed over time, but back then parents told their kids as little as possible and rebuked questions they didn't like.

Later that morning we arrived in Fort Towson, Oklahoma. Located in Choctaw County, it is a small place with only a few hundred souls living there. Named for a hero of the War of 1812, it was established as a fort in 1824. The town came into existence in 1902, shortly before Nanny and Poppa stayed there briefly. It sits on the flat wooded plains on Eastern Oklahoma. It was a sunny and hot day. But we were not there to visit anyone in the town or its landmarks. We were there to find a grave.

We found the cemetery or at least one of them. We got out of the station wagon and went walking among the graves. So far in our young lives we had not actually been inside many graveyards, so to say the least it was quite spooky and unsettling. Poppa paced around and took off his felt hat and wadded it in his big brown hands in frustration. The other adults spread out and looked at the many old tombstones. Some of the dates said the dead people were born in the 1700's. Bewildered by this odd errand, we watched, hoping for a conclusion soon so we could eat something. It felt like we were there all day but I'm sure we were there only a few hours. Poppa started to cry as the day went on and Nanny stoically took him back to the car. We drove away in silence. I'm not sure we stopped and got any food, but I was glad when we were headed home. Home is where life made sense back then. It was years later when Nanny told me why we made the futile trip.

Nanny and Poppa had nine children and two died. One was a little girl who only lived a week. The other was Virgie Hancock and she was three when she fell sick. At some point they transitioned from a horse and wagon to a car, but when this tragedy occurred, they still moved around in a wagon, just like their forefathers did. Thus far their young family was Thelma, Alvis and then little Virgie. By now they reasoned they knew how to take care of them and do what was best. The wagon had a covering like the Conestogas the pioneers drove across wild America, but it was a bad time to be traveling. The wind was cold with sheets of rain mixed with ice and somewhere along the way Virgie got sick. Poppa was taking them to an oil field where his father and brothers had found work and were busy building wooden derricks for the drilling companies. Poppa was anxious to earn a decent paycheck and every day they spent getting there was a day's wages lost. It was a hard and desperate time. As he drove in the pouring rain with a sick child and a wife who was worried one of her kids was getting worse, they saw a house with a light on. They had arrived a few miles from the tiny town of Ft. Towson. The folks who lived inside the house were hospitable and offered them shelter, food and a place to sleep for a few days. The rains kept a steady downpour, but Virgie seemed better. Poppa wanted to go and complete the trip so he could start work. Nanny disagreed but Poppa won out and thanked the family who helped them and loaded them up and took off for the oil fields. Virgie died the next day. Now she may have passed anyway while they were in the warm dry cabin. Nanny blamed her husband and he agreed. He found some lumber and built her a crude casket.

In those days when someone died you seldom had the money to call the undertaker (if there even was one). The man of the house built a casket and dug a grave, while the wife washed her dead child and dressed them for burial. In the HBO series Deadwood, Sheriff Bullock's son is killed by a wild horse and they have the funeral inside their home. The process you see the Bullocks go through is what my grandparents went through more than once. They buried her in the Ft. Towson cemetery and Poppa made a wooden marker and carved Virgie's name on it. After some prayers were said and quite a bit of weeping was done, they loaded up with one less soul and set out for the oil fields.

As a father, I cannot imagine a harder event than to outlive one of your children, much less feel responsible for their demise. Nanny and Poppa carried this weight the rest of their days until Poppa got up one day and decided to make an effort to go back and see the grave of his daughter. Nanny stoically went with him and helped him look. I'm kind of glad we didn't know what was going on that day in Fort Towson. Poppa's grief came out full force and he paced all over this ill kept cemetery. Little Virgie's remains lay somewhere close by, but we were never able to find exactly where. Time and decay had rotted his grave marker years ago, but she would always be remembered. As David and I recalled that day and how we felt, some of worry and grief stayed with us sixty years later.

I don't know what lessons we gained from this except maybe that some things never stay in past, good and bad, but you carry them through out your days. We call them regrets and I think all of us have some if we are humans after all.

Poppa was born Thomas Asbury Hancock on November 3, 1888, in Cooke County, Texas. His father, Benjamin, was 32, and his mother Alvertine, was 34. Benjamin was a Methodist circuit rider on Sundays and a farmer the rest of the time. Poppa was raised in a large family where hard work was expected and the gospel was preached. Religion played a large part of Poppa's heart and outlook on life. Yes, his father was an old timey hell fire and brimstone preacher. However, Poppa talked more about the grandeur of the Almighty and the vast love God had for us. Raised on a farm, he learned how to make his way on his own. On one census when he was eleven, he is listed as a "farm laborer" even though he had older sisters who also worked in the fields, ages thirteen and sixteen. They were listed as "no occupation". When he was nine, one of his tasks was to call the cows in the evening and feed them. He would bang on the bottom of a bucket and they would form a line and head to the troughs in the barn. He noticed one evening they were making a crook in the march toward the feed, as if they were avoiding something. Young Tom ran down to see what they were sidestepping. It was a giant rattlesnake coiled and threatening to strike as the cows neared. Poppa knew he had to do something. He always carried a small rope in his back pocket. He took it out and made a noose on one end and roped the big snake after a few tries. He cinched the rope and not knowing what else to do, he took off running in a coming darkness. Poppa ran for at least a mile. Out of breath and adrenalin he stopped and bent over with his hands on his knees. Whipping up some last-minute courage, he turned to see what had become of the poisonous reptile. It was dead. Poppa had dragged it to death. Victorious, he ran back home and showed it off to his dad and mother. His father held it up to the top of his head and the tail touched the ground.

Poppa married Neoma "Oma" Jones on January 29, 1909. She was eighteen but Poppa fibbed on his age and told them he was twenty-one. He was actually twenty, but he needed his parents' permission unless he was twenty-one. Women could marry at eighteen. Poppa was nine months short, however this was a common practice at the time and the authorities turned a blind eye to it. His draft registration cards were revealing as he was fifty-three in 1941 the last time he registered. In WWI his draft card read "If a person is of African descent, tear off this corner". After they were wed, they moved around Oklahoma in a wagon as their children were born and finally settled in south western Oklahoma. They bought a farm a few miles from Apache, near Fort Sill and Lawton. It was here he and Nanny built their lives and their family on a farm. Most of his beloved stories began here. The first book I wrote contained a poem called "Virgie's Grave".

Virgie's Grave

She was so small when they had to put her to rest
From the back of a wagon, she had died in her nest
Ft. Towson's pines watched her leave the earth and escape
They guarded her tomb and made sure she was safe
The words were spoken and filled each others' hearts

She was so loved and cared for, why did she so soon depart?
We looked and we searched, no landmark could we find
She was here, so close, she was gone, it seemed so unkind
What if we had: would it be so important to us now?
A great mystery, so lovely, is living with us now
I'll never forget that day, when it was revealed to me
That one of us was here- but not for our eyes to see

STORY THREE

Geronimo and Frank James

Nanny and Poppa's house on West Dubois gave David and I a sense of freedom, love and adventure we didn't quite replicate anywhere else. All of the hundreds of meals we ate there with just our two grandparents usually consisted of food grown a few yards away that we helped plant, water and harvest. Fried squash and okra would be joined by corn on the cob and mashed potatoes and gravy. Nanny's homemade bread was sliced thick and smeared with real butter. Watermelon or cantaloupe would round out desert and then Poppa would pour honey or black molasses over a hunk of butter and sop it up with more yeast bread (Nanny's name for her bread opposed to store bread). Nanny would clear our plates away and stand at the sink and wash up quietly as Poppa would roll a Bull Durham and light it. He would blow a thick cloud and let his eyes look up at the ceiling. Many times, we knew this was a prelude to a story. "Dr. John, Nicodemus...did I ever tell you boys of the time I went to see Geronimo?"

Now, Poppa only told this story once or twice, but even as only grade schoolers, we definitely knew who Geronimo was, thanks to television and movies. So, we often would ask him to retell it just to make sure we understood what happened. It was a fairly short story, but it has lasted us through the decades.

History tells us that Geronimo was born in what we call Arizona today in the upper Gila River country. He was named Goyahkla, or "one who yawns". His tribe, the Bedonkohe, was part of the Chiricahuas, who in turn was under the umbrella of the Apache. As he grew into manhood, the Apaches were in a fierce war with Mexicans on the South, the U.S. Government to the North and neighboring Comanche and Navajo tribes. By the time he was 17, he had led four successful raids on the nearby tribes. His hatred of any kind of interference or dominion by outsiders was tempered while was went on a trading mission and came home only to find that Mexican soldiers, led by Colonel Jose Maria Carrasco had attacked his camp and murdered his wife, Alope, their three children and his mother.

Following Apache custom, he burned down all his family's possessions and retreated into the woods. After a time of reflection, he claimed to have heard a voice telling him that no bullets would ever slay him, and the voice would guide his arrows. He hunted down the killers and vowed to spend the rest of his life avenging them. There is not a definitive answer as to how he was called by the name we know. There are many tales but mostly unproven. It is possible Geronimo is just a bad pronunciation of Goyahkla. His name was used widely by paratroopers in WWII when they jumped and yelled "Geronimo!" referring to his bravery.

Western expansion doomed Native Americans, but the Apache fought on and escaped capture so often he embarrassed the U.S. Army. In March of 1886, General Crook forced him to surrender, but at the last minute, Geronimo and forty of his men escaped in the dark. They were pursued by thousands of soldiers, both Mexican and American. His band of loyalists sometimes rode seventy miles per day to avoid capture. This went on for five months and finally the Apache turned himself in on September 4th, 1886. He and his soldiers were sent to Fort Pickens, Florida by train, and then loaded and sent to Mount Vernon Barracks in Alabama. They were finally sent to prison at the Comanche and Kiowa reservation near Fort Sill, Oklahoma, where Poppa happened to be at that point. Geronimo spent fourteen years at Fort Sill. He was eventually approved to leave on trips to World Fairs and Wild West Shows. He participated in Theodore Roosevelt's inauguration, but President Roosevelt refused his plea to allow he and his tribe to return to their native lands.

Geronimo died of pneumonia at Fort Sill on February 17, 1909. He was buried at the Beef Creek Apache Cemetery in Fort Sill. Poppa must have been a young man when he encountered Geronimo, as he was twenty years old when he died. Poppa found out Geronimo was there in the Fort Sill prison and wanted to see him and have a conversation with the great man. He was locked away when Poppa met him and sitting on the floor of his cell. I asked Poppa once how he was able to go into the jail and meet him. Poppa simply said, "I just asked them if I could." He said the great warrior was sitting there and combing his hair. I don't recall the specifics of what they talked about, but Poppa came away with a feeling of sadness as that was how he said Geronimo seemed to him.

Our Poppa was enamored by Native Americans and their way of life. He was happy that several tee pees were pitched on his farmland. My mother told stories of how as a child she would be playing and suddenly look up and a man in Native dress would be standing a few feet away. She would never hear a sound of them coming up to the house to see her father. Nanny even named her after a woman whose tee pee she would visit – Muriel. Both of our grandparents would come to know many of these Native Americans and respect their customs, foods and ideas.

On many occasions Poppa would take out his old Barlow knife and teach us how to whittle and play mumbly peg and other tricks. I would often try to mimic his skills cutting wood and end up cutting the hell out of my fingers as the sharp knife would slide easily through the wood and stab my other hand and fingers. Once while Poppa was demonstrating this, David and I asked about the Geronimo story and after Poppa told us this now familiar tale, he kept on whittling and casually mentioned "You know, I met Frank James, too."

The James brothers' father was a Baptist preacher who moved with his wife, Zelda, from Kentucky to Missouri. Frank was the eldest and when he was eighteen, he joined the Missouri State Guard. The James family was living in the heavily Confederate western side of the state. When Union troops overtook Lexington, Frank became sick and was left behind as the Confederate army retreated. He surrendered to the Union and eventually made to sign an oath to the Union forces. In the state of Missouri, a conflict arose between bands of Pro-Confederate irregulars

(Bushwhackers) and the Union home guards. The home guards were tracking down the leader of one of the guerrilla bands and raided the Samuel farm (Frank's stepfather) and tortured the man trying to find the location of the guerillas. Frank had become an active member of one such band and after the raid joined Quantrill's company and took part in the Lawrence Massacre in 1863 when over 200 locals were killed. Later he was sent to prison and was paroled. After he was freed Frank was tangled up in a gun fight in Brandenburg, Kentucky where two soldiers were killed, and Frank was shot in the hip. Shortly after this, he and his brother, Jesse, formed a band of outlaws and began robbing banks.

There are way too many movies and TV shows to list here that recount the infamous James Gang. Joe Walsh once led a very fine rock band named after them. Jesse James lives in the American memory of the Wild West. Many of the stories told about their exploits are pure fiction but we love a good outlaw tale. Five months after Jesse was killed in 1882, Frank James boarded a train and headed to see the Governor in Jefferson City, Missouri. He had an appointment and when he got to his office, he placed his gun in Governor Crittenden's hand and said "I have been hunted for twenty-one years, and have literally lived in the saddle, and have never known a day of perfect peace. It was one long, anxious, inexorable, eternal vigil. Governor, I haven't let another man touch my gun since 1861."

His New York Times obituary recounts this part of his life.

"In 1882, Frank James surrendered in Jefferson City, Missouri. After his surrender he was taken to Independence, Missouri and held in jail there for three weeks. He was later moved to Gallatin, Missouri, where he remained in jail for a year, awaiting trial. Finally, he was acquitted and went to Oklahoma to live with his mother. He was never in the penitentiary or convicted of the charges against him."

As David and I discussed which stories to include in the book, we had little difficulty what stood out over the test of time and stories that had drifted into lost memories. Telling how our grandfather met two of the most famous characters of all time was an easy decision. However, the actual writing of these was much harder as we had so little details. We grew up in an age where adults did most of the talking and our job was to listen, not be heard. We both wish now we would have broken that rule and asked a lot more questions. Poppa told us he met Frank James at either a bank or the courthouse in Lawton. We don't recall which. He said he knew who he was and when he got the chance, he greeted Mr. James and shook his hand. That was about it. We weren't too interested in being 100% factually correct in the book. It is mainly based on our aging memories. However, before letting the Frank James story get into print, I just wanted to see. Did Frank James ever come to Oklahoma? Could have Poppa really met the famous outlaw? There was no question about Geronimo as it is a historical fact, he was incarcerated at Fort Sill.

But Frank James? I knew little to nothing about him but dug quietly into a Google search and found the above obituary in the New York Times which mentioned him living in Oklahoma. The more I searched I found dozens of Old West sites with plenty of Frank James stories. Some may even be true.

I finally found the following article in the Oklahoman Archive from July 25, 1909. when Poppa was almost twenty-one. "Frank James, formerly a member of the famous James brothers, who committed numerous depredations in Missouri and terrorized citizens throughout the middle west, is certainly a man of his word. Soon after Jesse James was killed and Frank James surrendered to the Governor of Missouri, the chief executive promised him a pardon, provided that he, Frank James, would live a "quiet and peaceful life". Frank promised to follow his instructions which he has done. James and his wife moved to a farm near Fletcher in southwestern Oklahoma in 1906. There they raise chickens and corn on 100 acres of land. Mr. and Mrs. James attend church and social gatherings and Mr. James is ranked as one of the foremost men in that part of Oklahoma. A great many people stop at Fletcher to visit the once noted outlaw. They are always tendered a cordial welcome and are asked to remain as long as they like, provided they do not get too inquisitive about Mr. James' past life. Mr. James seldom refers to his reckless Missouri days and is sensitive towards publicity. One of the principal reasons why he moved to the farm was to evade so much newspaper notoriety and the very curious public."

In 1911, Frank James's mother, Zelda Samuels, died on a train near Oklahoma City en route from Fletcher to visit her grandson. Shortly after her death, Frank and his wife moved from Oklahoma, eventually returning to his farm at Excelsior Springs, Missouri.

Fletcher is sixteen miles from Apache, and they are both twenty miles north of Lawton.

STORY FOUR

The Doctor's Office

In mid 2020 David and I were in an hour-long telephone call sharing our respective views on what had transpired so far in a dumpster fire of a year. Toward the end of the conversation, I was getting hungry and noticing the clock in our two-hour time difference. As I was saying goodbye, he thought of something and asked me to hear him out. He said, "I've got a story about Poppa you don't know." Of course, I wanted to hear it, so he recounted a time when he was a young lad and our mother made him get dressed and accompany her to take her father and mother to visit his physician in downtown Denison. I listened to the very old news of how Poppa reacted in a socially awkward situation and smiled. This definitely sounded like Poppa. After David was done, he went on to number all the other stories of Poppa's life we were a part of and some only we had heard him tell. David ended the call by simply stating "We should write a book."

Later on, that evening after a chicken dinner and sipping a cocktail, my thoughts went back to our conversation. I lost track of what was happening on Netflix and could see Poppa in that doctor's office in the early 1960's. I remembered the office and how it looked. I also remembered the times and how strange they seem now. I shook it off and rewound the episode to catch up on what I missed. The next several days I was troubled by this idea of a book about Poppa. Neither of us cared about having a wide readership. We only knew that if we didn't write these tales down, they would be lost forever. Forever. That would be a shame. So, this is the story that gave lift off to this book. Since it is David's memory at work here, I will let him tell it.

I could already read and write so I must have been seven or eight years old. We got up early and got to scurrying around. It must have been 1962 or 63. I don't know why momma made me go, maybe Poppa wanted me to. I believe it was in the summertime and momma washed my face, and I had on short pants. Momma didn't like the shirt I picked out and made me take it off and choose another one. Momma never said a word to me about what we were doing. So, we drove down the hill from Amsden to pick them up. Poppa was already on the porch waiting for us. We didn't even get out of car. Poppa gathered Nanny up and came and got in the car with us. We drove downtown and parked on Main Street near the Bear Building. Bear Drugs had a lunch counter in the front with a soda fountain and ice cream. The drug store was at the back and there were steps or an elevator to take you up to the second floor where the Doctors' offices were. "

Before we get to what happened next, I need to give some background on where this took place. Downtown Denison. Our downtown was much like all American Main Streets in small towns in the 1950's and 60's. Downtown was the heart, soul, bones and lifeblood of our lives back then. On Main Street you found anything you could ever want. Our junior high school was at one end and already surrounded by tire stores, insurance companies, funeral parlors, and grocery stores. Watsons Hamburgers was across the street and held the center of teen social life.

Walk a few blocks and there was Ashburn's Ice Cream and Barrett Drugs, where you could buy anything from wedding rings to shotguns. The Rialto Theater was where we would see all of the movies that would change our world views and took a date on Friday night. On weekend nights people under twenty-five would cruise the night away and listen to the loud radios and hot rods trying to impress the impressionable. A few years ago, I wrote a poem describing those days.

I Remember Denison (In Its Hey Day)

I remember Denison in its hey day...and
the intense excitement on Christmas mornings

Golden Rule School days – fresh wax on the wood floors

I remember Denison in its hey day ...and
waiting for endless Katy rail cars to pass us
the signal rang loud

Burns Runs summers – Mrs. Cooke's eight grade
History class

I remember Denison in its hey day ...when
all the factories were running

Dragging Main on Friday nights – chrome
engines humming

I remember Denison in its hey day ... when eight
tracks and mini skirts came to town

My first encounter with The Beatles – and learning
their songs

I remember Denison in its hey day ...when
all the stores were open (barber shops too)

I remember Watsons ...and McDaniel Junior High School
and Saturdays at the Rialto

I remember the Safeway plant ...where my daddy used to
work

Driving downtown on Armstrong Avenue and buying gas
for twenty-five cents

I remember Sundays and eating Ashburn's Ice Cream
Bomb shelter drills ...polio sugar cubes
Long summer dreams
I remember Sid Maples and my first good guitar
Fishing in the winter
Heading to Dallas that seemed so far away

I remember the first time I fell in love there ...
and smaller clothes that fit me

I remember Denison in its hey day and when I wanted
to leave and explore the world

But looking backward brings a sweet feeling and an
appreciation for its hold on me then

David continues the story: "We rode the elevator up to
where the Doctor's offices were and went inside. Nanny
and Momma went up to the counter to get Poppa checked
in and Poppa held my hand and led me over to where the
seating area and chairs were located. There was a sign on
the wall that said, "Colored Section". Poppa stood there
and looked at it for a long pause, maybe thirty seconds or
more, which was a long time for Poppa. He took me over

to where that section was, and we sat down in it. I saw there was two water fountains; one said "Whites" and the other said "Colored". Now, I could read the words he read but didn't understand what it meant. Nanny and Momma gave him dirty looks for breaking the rules but didn't mention it out loud. I thought about this incident my whole life. When Poppa got through with his appointment and we rode home nobody said a word about him wanting to sit in the "Colored Section". This was a time when there were beginning to show on TV the marches. People were marching in Memphis and Mobile. They marched on Washington. This was all for voting rights. I was older when I understood what Poppa was doing. It dawned on me again in 2020 when George Floyd was killed. Poppa was the first white person I knew whose life said, "Black Lives Matter". He was friends with Cleo Wolf, a full blood Indian. Cleo was a welcome guest at Poppa's dinner table. They hunted coons together. He was friends with Norman Caruthers, a man who was mildly mentally disabled and threw the Grit Newspaper. In other words, Poppa was friends and liked people who made those around him uncomfortable."

As David shared this memory with me, both of us recalled his hands. David remembered Poppa taking him by the hand when they got off the elevator and went in the Doctor's Office. His big old brown hand led him over to the "Colored Section". God only knows the wars with mother nature those hands had fought. The Great Depression and the Dustbowl farm on his Oklahoma land were visible in his hands. Several years ago, I wrote a poem simply about his hands.

I Held His Hand

They were large and brown,
                    much bigger than mine

They held a plow for so
                    long, they seemed to incline

The hands they had shaken, the
                    hammers they had grasped

Had come to reside
                    in the scars at last

Indians and Outlaws had all
                    crossed his path

Winters and Summers stormed
                    with their wrath

His back was still straight,
                    his eyes gleamed deep blue

He spoke with Authority
                    his enemies were few

I followed his footsteps
                    down fresh broken earth

Watching green corn
                    inch up from their birth

He told me stories
                    and gave me a heart

He always included me -we were

> Never apart

He made me feel proud to call

> me his own

That feeling still comes, when

> I kneel at his headstone

He's gone and went to a

> faraway land

What keeps my faith strong is

I held his hand

STORY FIVE

The Mule

David says this is his favorite story. I think it's might as well, because it exposes the earthy quality of Poppa and our lives as 901 West Dubois. I was present for this event, but like the concrete porch, I arrived just as it was beginning. David Bucher (Nicodemus) has the complete report.

"I had spent the night there with Nanny and Poppa. He got me up really early. I knew he was jazzed about something, but I didn't understand exactly what it was. We wolfed down our breakfast and went outside to the north garden and started looking down Scullin Street to the north. We stayed out there hunkered down and looking down the street. He finally told me we were going to have a man come up and plow up the garden. I didn't have any idea what that entailed. I didn't know what that was all about. I did not know the implements we were going to use. I saw Daddy out there sometimes using that old hand plow you pushed. We never did own a tiller. The man next door bought one and it nearly made Poppa cry. So, way in the distance you could see a man in a wagon with a mule pulling it. They were coming over Star Street and toward us. Poppa stood up and started walking back and forth and I could tell he was excited. The man drove the wagon off the street and up the alley by the big old pine tree. He stopped the mule and got down from the wagon. He and Poppa talked for a while about what Poppa wanted. They shook hands and that was that.

Poppa pushed the fence down and stepped over it and went into the alley to the wagon. Him and the old man took a big breaking plow off the wagon and set it down. They lifted the breaking plow over the fence and sat it down inside the garden. I said to myself this is cool; this is going to be good. It looked really neat. I was little, maybe five years old. So, the old man had big ass blanket, like a giant furniture company has to move furniture. They placed the furniture blanket over the fence, and I noticed the mule looked at that blanket. The old man goes around and unhitches the mule and brought him around to where that cover was laying. He said something to the mule and for a while it seemed he and the mule were talking. The mule stepped sideways across the fence, left to right to where the blanket lay and stood perfectly still in the garden. The old man went back to the breaking plow and reached down and hooked the plow to the mule. Then he spoke to the mule a little bit more and took the reins in his hands and laid them on the frame of the breaking plow. He spoke to the mule once more and there he went- off he goes! I'm little and they start turning dirt and I don't have anything to compare it to. It was MONSTER. The furrows were huge with big piles of brown dirt. He then stopped and asked, "Is this all right, Mr. Hancock?" Poppa replied, "A little deeper."

He pushed down harder on the plow and spoke to the mule and MAN! They pushed some dirt. They went down the rows and turned as they got close to the fence so he could let the mule go. He was making complete circles. Poppa got on to me for getting too close so I had to find a place in the corner so I could squat down and watch.

I was not missing this shit when I saw this happening. They made another pass and I'm hunkered down by the old pear tree and the old man keeps talking to the mule and the mule makes a noise and they keep going round and round. I thought "man this is something". It seemed like they went at it for a long, long time, but it probably wasn't. So, they plowed the north garden and that was a full city lot. The west garden was two city lots.

They disconnected the mule and took that big old mule through the gate by the carport and into the west garden. The man and Poppa pulled up that huge steel plow and I think the mule helped skid it along on the ground. The west garden was twice as big as the other garden and had peach and plum trees in it. It was the same drill. The man and the mule went at it and Poppa said, "a little bit deeper". Poppa wanted every penny for his plow fee. Just like the concrete. When they started plowing behind the little house, Nanny came out in the mix. She knew they were getting close to her polk bushes. One was by the pear tree and another one in the west garden was by the strawberry bed in the old boat. She told Poppa "Tom, you better save my polk bushes." But Poppa kept telling the man "Nope, get closer to the boat." Nanny was pissed. She got out there and started pulling at the sides of her dress and waving at the mule not to plow over her polk bushes. Just then the man plowed right through her polk. She was mad. She went over to that big polk bush and pulled it up. It was over waist high. She told all of them off, the old man, Poppa, and the poor old mule. She went to find a new place for her polk bush. It must have been early spring. Nanny came back in a little while and told me to get back in the house. I told her I thought they needed me out here. So, I stayed and watched as they kept plowing the west garden and Poppa kept saying "a little deeper". When they were done it was like something on TV. It looked wonderful. I saw things that day my children will never see, unless they go to Silver Dollar City or something like that. But man, they plowed that garden up. When they were done, they went back up to the north garden. He unhitched the mule. The man and Poppa set the plow back over the fence and put the blanket back on the fence. The mule stepped sideways again only this time it was from right to left. The old wagon he had was a real old timey wagon, except it had car tires on it. I saw that man a few more times around the Cotton Mill area. The furniture blanket kept the mule calm and not afraid of the fence."

As a wide-eyed kid, I witnessed probably ninety percent of his account, but it was enough to last a lifetime. I arrived about the time the mule was tip toeing over the fence. I don't think either one of us had seen a mule up close before. One of our uncles had horses and we had ridden them, but a mule was different. Plus, this one had a task that he knew how to achieve. It was huge. Unlike my brother I had no idea what was about to occur. It was like a spaceship had landed. The plow looked as big as a ship! It compared to a cow catcher on a locomotive train with dual wooden handles attached to the steel behemoth.

Poppa didn't take the back fence by the alley completely down, he sort of bent it over. This was very disconcerting as it seemed like a wall in a house had fallen. The north garden was mostly for corn. In the west garden Nanny raised cucumbers, pea vines, purple hull peas, onions, tomatoes and squash. She canned most of this and we ate some of it fresh daily. And yes, she had polk bushes. This was the only time we could remember Poppa hiring someone to plow the garden. All the other years they used a metal push plow that had handles and a wheel. It was tough work.

The book is about Poppa, but Nanny carries as much room in our minds and hearts as he did. She was born Neoma Jones on February 17, 1890, in Alvord, Texas. She said her family had migrated from Kentucky at some point by wagon. Her mother was Ella (Hooker) Jones, and her father was William B. Jones. When she was just a girl, her family was camped along a trail and some men came through one night and got into an argument with her father. They were drunk and slammed a large ceramic whiskey jug over his head and killed him as she watched in horror. Later her mother married a man named Gray and Nanny always referred to him as Mr. Gray. The only close relative of hers we knew was a brother James, or "Uncle Jimmy" as my mother called him. He, like his sister was a sweet and generous man. I was invited to accompany him once to a cattle auction near Frederick, Oklahoma. Afterward he drove out in the country and showed me a tract of land he owned. I saw cows grazing on it and a few oil wells pumping. Nanny taught me to read the Denison Herald Newspaper before I went to the first grade. David and I loved to sit in her kitchen and watch her bake bread. Once I came in the front door and the entire front room was filled with a quilting frame suspended in the air and Nanny was diligently stitching the colorful patches.

When I was in the eighth grade, I was assigned to interview someone who lived through the Great Depression. I went to Nanny. In her soft voice she said "Oh, it just wasn't that bad. We could grow much of what we needed and would trade with their neighbors for what they could provide. We just didn't have any actual money. Nobody did." I asked her about the Oklahoma Dust Bowl that they had to endure as well. She smiled and said that Poppa went to the Department of Agriculture and got help with farming techniques such as terracing. However, she did not like Herbert H Hoover. She told me HHH stood for Hoover, Hell, and Hard times.

STORY SIX

James Westbrook and Sweet Potatoes

Our young lives were formed by being at 901 West Dubois. Most of Poppa's neighbors were never in much contact with us. The one exception was James Westbrook. He lived across the street and east half a block. In his younger days, Westbrook was a Texas Ranger. In 1823, Stephen F. Austin founded the Texas Rangers as a paramilitary force to protect the new settlers who came out to Texas following the Mexican War of Independence. The Rangers fought the Comanche and Cherokee tribes who called Texas home. The Rangers grew from ten to fifty to one hundred and fifty men by 1841. They established a fearsome presence with a few famous warriors such as John Coffee "Jack Hays, Ben McCullough, Big Foot Wallace, and Samuel Hamilton Wallace. They prevented the assassination of William Howard Taft and Portofirio Diaz in El Paso and were involved in some of the Old West's best known criminal cases. They hunted John Wesley Harding, Sam Bass, and Bonnie and Clyde. The Lone Ranger television series was loosely based on the Texas Rangers and Texas named one of their Major League Baseball teams after them. There is a museum in Waco dedicated to them.

Jim Westbrook was a big man, large. His voice was loud, partially due to him being hard of hearing, but also because he seemed to loom large in spirit as well as in body. He wore striped overalls and a white shirt. He dipped snuff and had drippings leaking out both sides of his mouth. He lived alone and liked to listen to the radio and occasionally the television. He must have loved to watch *I Love Lucy* because we could hear it clearly inside

Poppa's house when it was on. Mr. Westbrook (Nanny told us to call him that) enjoyed walking up to Poppa's house using a wooden cane and talking at length about their lives. We would sit with Nanny in the kitchen when they talked, and she would whisper to us what the men were discussing and explain parts of it in kid language.

David and his buddy Randall Hughes liked to hang out down at the old Ranger's house and listen to him talk. One Christmas, the boys got brand new air rifles and decided to go on a hunt. They prowled around Nanny and Poppa's house for a while and ended up in the vacant wooded and overgrown lot behind Westbrook's home. They spent half the day shooting at anything they could find. They grew tired of big game hunting and exited beside Mr. Westbrook's fence. Big Jim saw the boys and asked them what they were up to? They confessed to bird hunting and gave him the bad news of coming up empty handed. He invited them up to his porch and the boys now worried they might be in some kind of trouble. Westbrook took one of their guns and as he examined it, he told them how once he shot the crown out of a Mexican's hat when he was a Texas Ranger. The Mexican Revolution erupted along the Texas border between 1910 and 1920. The Governor of Texas called upon the Rangers to ride down there and fight and fight they did. It was a bloody mess. Many of James Westbrook's sagas were soaked in the bloody fighting there.

Uncle Jim told David and Randall if they would go into his kitchen and find some wooden kitchen matches and stick some in a fence post he would light them by shooting so close the heat from the bullet would light the match. Lighting matches by a bullet! Hells bells not even the Lone Ranger could do that! The boys scurried in the kitchen and brought out a hand full of loose matches. In those days it was common for most kitchens to have readily available matches to light the stove burners or the oven. Westbrook told the lads where to stick the matches into the wood fence post that was laced with hog wire near a small gate. The fence posts were made of old railroad ties and had deep crevices. The boys retreated back on the porch and Uncle Jim asked them how the rifle operated and after a minute he understood. Now, the old Ranger had never seen these air rifles before and had never even touched one. He fired and the boys raced off the porch to inspect the target matches. He failed to light the match but shot the tip head of the match clean off. The boys were amazed. He instructed them to place another into the post. He shot the air rifle three of four more times. He never was able to light the match head but knocked the head off several matches.

Randall Hughes and David Bucher were marked by the demonstration and looked for more evidence of his stories to solidify his Ranger legacy. They couldn't find many resources at that time in life. David admits to not being as tenacious as Randall was. One afternoon, when the pair shared an hour in the library at McDaniel Junior High, in downtown Denison, Randall sat across a table from David and had been digging diligently in a pile of old books.

He grew excited and yelled at David to come over on his side of the table to see what he had found. The librarian shooshed at them to quiet down. Randall pointed to a picture in a book he had found about the Texas Rangers. The old black and white photograph depicted a string of horse mounted Rangers in cowboy hats. Under the picture their names were printed. The third cowboy was a big fellow in a large hat. It read JAMES WESTBROOK.

In those days our parents didn't really care where we decided to spend our days as long as it was outside. A typical summer day would include a notion to go visit our grandparents and walk down the hill from Amsden Street, one and a half blocks to Dubois Street. Nanny was always glad to see us and was usually preparing the mid-day meal. One or two more plates were always ready and welcome. She would be baking several loaves of bread, slicing fresh tomatoes and cantaloupe, boiling corn, and mashing potatoes with butter and cream. A lot of their meals were purely vegetarian as they ate what they grew. She would tell me to go out to the garden and call Poppa in and we would eat. But first Poppa would pray over the waiting meal with words he had learned and heard many times from his father, Benjamin, the Methodist circuit rider. As a kid it sounded like he could actually see God and was talking directly to him.

Their gardens were a wonder. Corn, potatoes, okra, strawberries, blackberries, pears, walnuts, peaches, apricots, sweet potatoes, tomatoes, onions, various hot peppers, squash, eggs, watermelons, and honey all came from that soil and were displayed on their simple kitchen table. The only things my mother would go to Safeway and buy for them was things like, flour, yeast, sugar, butter, Crisco, coffee, tea, some cuts of meat. Those were the items they couldn't produce. One time I was horror struck as I came for a visit and Nanny was wringing two chickens' necks at the same time and the bloody headless birds were flailing all over the yard. But it was all part of the magic of my own flesh and blood who knew no other way of life, but to provide the best they could. Nanny and Poppa had spent most of their lives on a farm in western Oklahoma. When they were born electricity was new to that part of the world. They saw the arrival of automobiles, airplanes, television, telephones, paved roads, movie theaters, refrigeration, air conditioning, and most of the things we expect and take for granted. To David and me, the garden was a wonder.

I remember that Poppa wore the same kind of clothes almost every day. He put on blue overalls, a long sleeve shirt and wore a hat if he was outside (he had been bald for a long while by then). The hat was a faded felt one and had sweat stains inside the brim. He was tall to me, just under six feet. He was brown from working in the Oklahoma sun his entire life, but his upper arms were pale. He rarely wore a short sleeve shirt. He had blue eyes and loved to laugh. Nanny wore a dress every single day. They were her only clothes. Together they worked the land their entire life and thank God they did. Because in the early 1960's, Daddy transferred to Oakland, California, the hub of Safeway and all its offices and manufacturing plants. I loved living there, but Mom and Dad didn't, so after a year we returned to Texas. Broke. Our family was broke, and Daddy discovered he couldn't find a job for a while.

Things like this never troubled Nanny and Poppa. They went to work and planted. Poppa planted lots of different things as always, but this time he over did it on the sweet potatoes. He planted oodles of them, and God sent rain and sunshine so that their large green tops flourished and bloomed in the earth. There became hundreds, maybe thousands of perfectly good and edible sweet potatoes. Back then, about the only time we were served this food was at Thanksgiving. Usually, they were baked in a dish with marshmallows on top. This year was different. It began with harvest time and David Bucher was involved in this part of this unusual event.

Poppa used an ancient seed fork to uproot the ripe sweet potatoes. A seed fork is a farm implement that has four long slender metal fingers like a pitchfork but are not sharp. It bears a heavy oak handle that by this time was worn smooth. Poppa would shove the seed fork into the earthy garden dirt and uproot the oblong orange potatoes. David helped Nanny gather the dirty piles and brush them clean. They loaded them into the old wheel barrow (this was before it was used to carry the concrete) and Poppa would push it over to the east side of his house that had a small crawl space door that led into the dark room under that side of the house. The crawl door was small and the head room inside was only inches, so Poppa knew only one human who could fit in there and was also willing to complete the task. David crawled into the dark dirty unknown and waited as Poppa began to shove the sweet potatoes in the space and entrusted his grandson to make them all fit. His slim and agile body stacked rows and rows of them filling the dark space. David guessed there must have been thousands of them. He lined them up under the house for days and days. Little did he know that this was the food we would all eat for the rest of the year, along with the other fruits and vegetables the garden would yield.

In the movie Forrest Gump, Bubba recounts how many ways there are to serve shrimp. Nanny cooked sweet potatoes. Every day. We had sweet potatoes almost every meal. She made them mashed, boiled, baked, fried, and also pies from this abundant supply. Once she was watching a pie cool that was minutes out of the oven and offered me some. It looked like pumpkin pie. She added a dollop of whipped cream onto the slice, and I tasted it. I complimented her on the delicious pumpkin pie. She corrected me and said "No, it's sweet potato pie." To this day, David Bucher will not eat sweet potatoes in any form.

STORY SEVEN

Family Reunions and Searching for The Lost Dog

Tom Hancock had a large family as did most of his siblings. As the years went by, Poppa's brother George's wife, May, talked of getting the families that lived in that part of Oklahoma together once a year to at least see each other and visit. This was a time before technology provided any means of contact. The only avenue the ladies had was the U.S. Mail. Nanny and "Aunt May" (as our mother called her) were compelled to keep those ties that bind long after their children and distant relatives moved from the nest. There were plenty of Hancocks in Oklahoma and Texas and the response was good. After plenty of planning, "The Reunion" as it simply came to be known was settled in a campground in the Wichita Mountains Wildlife Refuge in western Oklahoma. As we grew up, this was a must attend annual event for the Bucher family. No tents were to be had just army cots and blankets. Everybody brought plenty of food (Hancocks were by trade farmers) and talking was the main event. There were no televisions, telephones, movies, or music. Just talk.

As a child I was in absolute wonder to be in the wildlife refuge. There were prairie dogs galore and their villages were dotted all over the land. But the main attraction was the buffalo, American Bison. Poppa would take me by the hand and lead me out to gaze at the herds. There they stood, majestic and proud, just like the westerns I had watched, only this was real. There they were! Alive and chewing their cud. They were also dangerous. One time a herd decided to run through our camp at night. It was an experience everybody talked about for decades.

Now, David and I didn't know who most of these people were, as they were our mother's cousins and relatives. They were nice to us and urged us to eat as much food as we wanted on those long tables weighted down by hams, fried chicken, watermelons, cantaloupes, various vegetables, desserts, and gallons of iced tea and Kool Aid. However, I did not need anyone to tell me how important our Poppa was to them. Tom Hancock was an elder statesman to this group of one hundred plus souls who expected him to sit in front of them and tell some stories. He did not disappoint.

On one such occasion, Ben Hancock, a nephew of Poppa's, somehow rigged a large reel to reel tape recorder to a power source and hung the microphone on a tree limb above Poppa's head. A crowd had gathered that night and Poppa was seated near a picnic table under a grove of oak trees. Lanterns were lit as Poppa told his many tales. Poppa had no clue he was being recorded and went on about a tale of coon hunting with his dogs at length. I don't think he owned any guns, so killing his prey was not the goal. It was the hunt. Poppa loved his hunting dogs, and his favorite sport was being in the woods with his hounds who caught the scent of a band of raccoons. The chase was afoot! He would spend all night running after them. When the hounds had treed a coon, then it was all over. Time to go home. One such night, it was a hot Oklahoma summer full moon hunt. Poppa could hear the dogs were barking and had went down a ravine near a creek. He followed them down the creek and was exhausted. He knelt down in his overalls and took his hat off. He bowed his head and scooped up water to drink from the running creek. His bald head was dripping with sweat as the southern moon gleamed a reflection off his shiny head. A large raccoon, that had eluded Poppa and his hounds, was sitting on a large overhanging branch above. The raccoon mistook Poppa's shiny head for a landing rock in the creek and jumped from the limb onto his head. The surprised animal was shocked at his mistake and fled upriver away from the hunters. Poppa was knocked out cold.

The next day, Ben Hancock sat Poppa down and played the tape of his hunting tale. Poppa was amazed hearing himself talk and asked Ben if he could record something else? Ben complied and Poppa commented on this newfound wonder. I am paraphrasing as it has been a long time since I heard his exact words of that tape, but this was the gist of it. "I listened to this tape recording and thought about it for a while. I thought about it quite a bit. I know that God has a tape recording of my whole life. I wonder if people would like to hear that tape recording? I don't think I want to people to hear that one because there are some things, I don't want folks to know about. However, I take comfort in knowing that the blood of Jesus Christ washes away all sins."

When Poppa moved to Denison, he left his farm behind, but he still made a large garden. He acquired new dogs and found new people to go hunting with. This story is one of David's earliest memories in his life. "I was real small and had spent the night with Nanny and Poppa. Poppa had gone coon hunting the night before with friends and they had brought several dogs. When the hunt was over, they blew the horns (coon hunters used carved cow horns and practiced blowing a loud "call to arms" sound) that signaled the dogs to come to the sound of the horns. All the dogs slowly returned, except one, a favorite of Poppa's. They blew several more times and waited but alas, the hound was not coming back. Poppa woke up that morning with an ache in his gut similar to the one that haunted him to seek Virgie's grave. Nanny made breakfast and as they finished, Poppa announced that he and his grandson were going back in the daylight to find his missing dog. As Poppa found David's small jacket, Nanny voiced her opposition to such an idea and strongly suggested he call our mother before tasking him on such an endeavor. Poppa waved off that idea by saying "Aww...she won't mind." This was said in the same spirit as Mac and the boys' idea in *Cannery Row*, when Mac suggested they take Joseph and Mary's old Model T on the frog expedition. Mac reasoned "He won't mind". The narrator adds "Not only did Joseph and Mary not mind, hell, he didn't even know."

The pair boarded Poppa's old Dodge, that was still running at the time. David was only four or five at the time and we don't recall any details about his car, except it was old. Real old. At that age, my brother had no real sense of where they were headed. He is pretty sure it was somewhere west of Sherman, way out in the country. Off they went! Poppa drove steadily with no drivers' license, his young grandson, and two fruit jars of well water. He was determined to find and bring that coon dog back home.

Poppa had no business driving at all, much less this far from DuBois Street, with only an enduring feeling of loss. David recalls they would stop along desolate country fence rows and Poppa would depart and blow that horn over and over. He would wait with David for a familiar yelp or sight of his missing hound. After nothing but a North Texas wind to blow across fields and woods, they would climb back in the old Dodge and drive further down a country road. He would stop every half mile or more and together they would walk hand in hand down the fence rows on both sides of the road. Poppa blew his hardest and called loudly for the dog. In a time with no cell phones or way to communicate, they worked the roads until way late in the afternoon. Poppa grew sadder and sadder. He and David were now hungry and tired. They walked miles and miles of country road. He would urge "Nicodemus, look on both sides of the road and keep calling the dog's name." David was equal to the task and was now invested in finding the dog as much as Poppa. At last, Poppa turned to David and said that they might as well call it day and come back tomorrow and resume their quest. David told him that sounded fine to him, they started back home.

When they pulled up into the carport at 901 West DuBois, everybody was present. Our parents and many of our relatives exhaled relief that the wonder boys had returned safely. Poppa casually complained that his car wasn't running very well and asked some of the men to take a look at it. Our dad, Leo Bucher and Albert Brinkley, a cousin, promised to work on it. They did, and it never ran again, ensuring Poppa's driving days were over.

STORY EIGHT

Zephyrinus Salinas

Most folks have heard of Pancho Villas but that's about it. You may be wondering why he would be in this story about our grandfather, but he did play a part in Tom Hancock's life. Chunks of the famous Mexican's history remains a mystery, but here's what we do know. He was born Jose Doroteo Arango Arambula on June 5, 1878. His father was a sharecropper and they lived on one of the largest haciendas in the state of Durango. Villa had four younger siblings. Only schooled enough for basic literacy, he quit school after his father died to help support his mother. Early on, he became a bandit while working as bricklayer, butcher and mule skinner. Eventually, he became a foreman for a USA railway company. When Villa turned sixteen, he returned to Durango to kill a landowner who raped his sister and fled on a stolen horse. Becoming a highway man along the hills, he joined a bandit band and went by the name Arango. In 1902 he was arrested by the Mexican police for stealing mules and assault. Forced into the army he wound up killing an army officer and stealing his horse. He was known then as Francisco "Pancho" Villa. He later joined the Mexican Revolution and sought to overturn the hacienda owners and the powerful politicians of President Diaz.

The revolution was a success, but the leader was not, and the cause was lost as the country struggled with war and violence for many more years. The wily Mexican fighter continued to play a part. Villa's army came into international fame in the years of 1913-1914. John Reed, the writer, spent four months with him and his soldiers and published burning accounts as a modern-day Robin Hood robbing the rich to give to the poor. In 1920, Villa retired from fighting and politics. The Mexican government gave him a hacienda in Chihuahua which he turned into a military colony. In 1923, he rejoined the political arena and was assassinated.

Poppa was a young father in Western Oklahoma farming his land near Apache. His oldest child, Thelma, was born in 1911. Like Poppa, she was put to work at a young age in the fields part of each day. It was how his father had raised him and those long before him. He taught her how to hoe the dirt in the crop rows and had sawed a hoe handle in half to make it her size. One day, Thelma was about six years of age, and was bent over cutting the earth with her mini hoe as Poppa watched her and did the same. The sun was early and bright as they labored under a blue sky. Suddenly, Poppa raised his head up to wipe the sweat from his brow and saw a man on a horse riding up the fence toward them. Poppa stopped working as the man grew closer. He was a Mexican soldier dressed in light colored clothing and a sombrero. He rode right up to them causing fear as to what his intentions were. The brown skinned man dismounted and instead of coming toward Poppa, he went over to little Thelma and took her small hoe out of her hands and made a motion in the air as to simulate what Poppa and his daughter were doing. He spoke these simple words "Me workee."

His name was Zephyrinus Salinas and Poppa let him work and live on his farm. I can't say how long Zephyrinus was around, but this had to have been around 1916 or 1917, and our mother was born in 1930. She remembered him well and spoke highly of him. He became a part of the Hancock tribe. He told Poppa he had indeed ridden with the famous outlaw, Poncho Villa, and had personally killed men as they fought. He said that was why he had run away to seek a new life. Zephyrinus said there just endless bloodshed and he grew weary of it. He sought to redeem himself and swore his loyalty to Poppa and his family. Whenever Poppa had to leave the farm on business for an extended time, he entrusted the safety of his loved ones to the old outlaw. Zephyrinus slept in the barn but ate his meals at their table.

Once, when Poppa had to go to Lawton to see a blacksmith, Zephyrinus accompanied him. For some reason, Poppa and the blacksmith began to argue over something. Zephyrinus didn't comprehend all of what it was about, only that his Patron and friend was being threatened or disrespected. In a flash, Zephyrinus produced a long sharp razor and suddenly grabbed the blacksmith by the hair of the head. He held the razor closely under the frightened man's throat and looked at Poppa. He waited for Poppa to give the word and the man's life was over, bleeding on the floor of the shop. This scared the hell out of our grandfather, and he assured Zephyrinus he wanted the man to be set free. Calmly, he let the man go and Poppa was in no doubt how far the man's love and loyalty would go.

Our family knows little more about this man who rode with bandits and freedom fighters. I was always intrigued by his name. Zephyrinus. I had never encountered the name in literature or stories. I dug a little when researching for this book and found a surprising clue. Zephyrinus was the Pope of Rome from 199 A.D. to 217A.D. He was head of the church at a time of great persecution by Emperor Severus. He was called "the holy pastor who was the support and comfort of the distressed flock." Like the namesake of this story there is less than a page or two written about him. My only guess is that Zephyrinus' parents were devout Catholic and were influenced by the history of their religion. Admirable!

STORY NINE

Cotton Mill Days and Honeybees

Our time growing up was when the Cotton Mill was running at a high capacity and was fully employed. It was built in 1890 and at that time it was the largest cotton mill west of the Mississippi. Cotton was king, but most of the men and women who toiled there were poor. The mill was a huge four-story brick building painted white with several towers. The smokestack was 170 feet high. It looked very old world industrial, that in 1937 produced 4.2 million yards of cotton material. By 1939, 225 souls worked there. By the early sixties most of them were on my paper route. I never set foot in there, but some of my relatives did, and every day I could hear the loud whistle blow anywhere I was in that part of town. The summer I was about to enter the eighth grade, Texas finally succumbed to the Federal law that integrated the school system. So, instead of continuing to attend Golden Rule, a county school provided for us that lived in the shadows of the Cotton Mill, we would be bused downtown to McDaniel Junior High. The first month, a guy I knew from Golden Rule came and sat next to me on the bus and asked "Hey, wanna be a paper boy?" Now, I had been reading the Denison Herald before I was sent to the first grade (Nanny taught me to read), and I looked forward to every afternoon (except Saturday) and waiting for the newspaper. The rolled-up newspaper would land in our yard and the daily events would unfurl on our kitchen table. I told him yes and I was thrilled. I had no idea what I was in for.

I was small for my age but had a bicycle and could ride fast. I got up early the following Sunday morning and rode over to his house which was a half block from Poppa's. In the dark we rolled about one hundred and ten giant Sunday Heralds and loaded them into a faded canvas saddlebag that hung off my handlebars on each side of the front tire. The bike was hard to pedal with all this unwieldy and heavy load. We then had to ride about six blocks over and down a hill to where the route started. I learned quickly to pedal forward, steer with my left hand and throw the paper on the lawn without tipping over. Some cranky old women wanted their paper on their porch and that was most difficult when their house was on a raised lot and built toward the back. Sometimes the paper landed on their roofs.

Delivering the Denison Herald was only half of the job back then. We were the collection agents for the business and after I got home from school, threw the one hundred plus newspapers, came back home and had supper, it was time to go back out there and ask these Cotton Millers to pay us. Homework would come later. The newspaper cost forty cents per week back then. The newspaper company got twenty-five cents and I got the remaining fifteen cents. I was given a binder with brown sheets of tear off "Paid" stickers that held the customer's name and address at the top. Those who were employed at the Cotton Mill got paid every two weeks on the first and the fifteenth. Their customer sheet had notes -1st and 15th. These hard-working citizens didn't have forty cents every week and paid me eighty cents twice a month. They were poor and I was a bill collector. I got to know the Cotton Mill very well. I knocked on every door once a week (more if nobody answered) and some folks peeked through the curtains and refused to answer. I would have to stop throwing their paper until they could pay me. Most folks were nice to me and were glad to pay me. There was no newspaper on Saturday and that was when I would count all the money and pedal downtown to pay the Herald. After that I would sometimes go to a movie.

Some of the houses were downright scary. Many of them were in bad disrepair and smelled bad when I knocked on the door. Mentally ill folks were kept at home, untreated and unsupervised, even the violent. But mainly it was the dogs. I can sympathize with the mail carriers. Occasionally I would encounter a frisky and loud barking pup, but there was one in particular. His name was Buster. He lived in one of those houses that sat up high off the dirt street and way back of the lot. It was a L shaped home with a porch that ran down most of the house. The house was unpainted, or so old the color was gone and was a faded rust. Lattice work covered the porch, and the lady insisted the paper be delivered on her porch. I tried a thousand ways to do that from my bike but not having a pitching arm for the Little League World Series, I surrendered to getting off the loaded bicycle and trotting up the porch and tossing it on her doorstep. Collecting the money was the biggest problem. I quickly discovered her dog, Buster, lived under the house and watched me.

It was in October, around Halloween, when he made his first move. On a cold spooky dark night, I dismounted and went to her porch. As soon as I knocked, I heard a sound under the porch. Buster moved fast bumping his head on the floor joists and entered the yard right by the steps. I turned to see what was going on as he ran to the far end of the yard and stopped. He paused and began running fast back toward the house. I don't remember the breed, color, or exact size he was. All I saw was what looked like an African lion coming to kill me. My heart was beating, and I trembled. There was no escape. Just as he was coming up the steps, the front door flew open, and the old lady saw me and her pet as he came close and yelled "Buster! Get back under the house!" The dog obeyed and my hands shook as I tore off her receipt. This happened every week afterward. Some weeks I didn't have the guts to endure this crap and didn't collect from her. I had nightmares all beginning with "what if?" What if the old lady wasn't home? What if she died? What if I got killed?

One day it happened. Buster was anxious to perform his routine and the old lady was slow to the door. I turned in horror as he was coming up the steps and he jumped up and knocked me down on the porch. He climbed on top of me and just before he tore out my throat, the old lady opened the door, saw the spectacle and shouted "Buster! Get off him!" The dog obeyed and I weakly got up. As she was fumbling in her purse to pay me and I was tearing off her receipt, I made up my mid. I was quitting today.

No more paper boy for me. It was too much. The old lady handed me a quarter, dime and a nickel and clucked wisely "Awww, you're afraid of Buster." "Yes ma'am, I am terrified of Buster." She replied something that changed my young life. "Buster ain't got no teeth. He got sick some time ago and they fell out." I didn't quit the Herald for another year and Buster somehow knew that I knew he was powerless against me. I learned that many things that cause us worry don't have any teeth.

In Poppa's west garden there were many fruit trees. Peach, plum and one large pear tree stood beside the little house. On the far western border of the west garden sat Poppa's Bee Super Boxes. Poppa was a beekeeper and a damn good one at that. There was always a jar of honey on his table to be poured on almost anything. The Supers huddled under a grove of fruit trees that the worker bees were seen flying around regularly. David and I kept away from these honey makers. As the garden grew and flowered, they went up and down the rows sucking nectar out. Inside the little house Poppa kept his tools for bee tending. He would don a straw hat with a metal screen that hung from the brim and protected his face and neck. The screen had a draw string he could tighten. Nanny would tie off his long sleeves and pants cuffs and Poppa would wear gloves as he handled a contraption that looked it like it belonged to the Tin Man in the Wizard of Oz. It was a metal container with a funnel for a top and an accordion like attachment hooked on its side that he would squeeze. I don't know what he would put inside but after he got it going, billows of dark smoke that held a strong smell would come out. Poppa said the "smoker" calmed the bees when it was time for him to rob the supers of their honey.

One time he got Daddy to borrow a truck and they hauled all of the bee boxes out by Lake Texoma to be near a field of grain so the bees would have plenty of pollen that year. He said it gave the honey a different taste. He claimed he rarely got stung and I don't recall seeing any bites on him. I, on the other hand, got stung plenty by the numerous yellow jackets and red wasps that enjoyed the fruit trees and vegetables in the garden. One morning after breakfast mom told me to go down to Poppa's house as David was already there helping capture a wild colony of bees. When I arrived, Poppa was putting an empty super under a peach tree as my brother sat near the tree beating a rhythm on the bottom of a bucket with a spoon. In the tree was a huge ball of buzzing bees. Poppa told me David's drumbeat calmed the bees and he planned on capturing and keeping them. It wasn't long before Poppa hit the tree hard and most of the bees fell off into the super. He quickly put the lid over it and smiled broadly as I got the hell away from it.

My most vivid memory was once when Poppa was going on a honey harvest and advised me to go in the house and shut the doors and windows. He put on his hat and gloves as Nanny tied him off. I turned on their small black and white television and got interested in whatever was being shown. After a few minutes I heard a commotion and looked outside the window. There was Poppa running wildly around the front yard with an entire beehive covering his head. The hat was nowhere to be seen as they clung to the outside of it making his entire head a cluster of bees. Two cedar shrubs stood on each side of the front porch and Poppa grabbed one of them and brushed it repeatedly against the bees trying to shake them loose. Eventually he did. Later he laughed about it as we ate hot baked bread with honey spread on it. He said "Doctor John, there were ten thousand bees out there and they were all mad at me. "

Ten Thousand Bees

They came in August, like an
army from the North:
      a large droopy bundle
      on a limb they held
      an old man's beard they
      became full of stingers and
      wings that beat

I ran out of breath to see them
like that, they pulsed, they moved
      as one they did think
      their center was lovely
      so strong and yet so weak
      they gave us their nectar
      we gave them our fear

the keeper came and told them to
wait, he was housing them soon:
      but they did not hear

> but they didn't know
> he was their friend

Ten thousand bees came to live
with us now, their ghost was gone
> so they wouldn't tame
> so we are their camp
> so they let us now dine
> honey and comb divine

STORY TEN

Murder In Mayberry

Facebook and other platforms of social media have brought the past alive with memories, old pictures, and grainy home movies. Those of us who are older love to recall how wonderful the past was and compare it to now. Us humans have a way of sanitizing the darker events and commit purposeful amnesia when talking about our school days. We post pictures of when we were young and talk about how dragging Main Street was the high light of life while we listened to eight track songs blaring out the windows of hot rods. American Graffiti (the movie) is how we see the past. Our hometowns become a make-believe Mayberry, where Andy, Opie, Aunt Bee and Gomer get along swell and if there is ever a problem, then good old Sheriff Taylor can fix it in a jiffy.

As David and I worked to collect what should and should not be in this book, we early on agreed to tell the dark stories that have stayed with us as well. Yes, growing up in Denison, at 901 West Dubois, at Nanny and Poppa's house was surely the most wonderful experiences we as children could have wanted. But there were some awful tragedies that happened too, and those events have stayed with us right along with the good ones. Our reasoning to include them was to look back and wonder how such brutal murders could occur in such a pastoral and idyllic chapter? We still wonder why? There were more killings that went on in Denison at the time but one of these hit close to home, our home.

Mr. and Mrs. W. J. Staton lived across the street and a little to the west of Nanny and Poppa's house at 918 West

Dubois. Our grandparents knew the Statons but that was about it. They were older (in their mid-eighties) and dirt poor. Mr. Staton was a retired farmer, and they were very religious and strict. However, they kept to themselves mostly and lived a quiet peaceful life. Their house wasn't much and was heated by a wood stove. Their rusty metal stove pipe would huff gray smoke during the cold Texas winters. We could see Mr. Staton feeding his chickens outside the chicken coop from Poppa's concrete porch. Halloween time was the only time I knocked on their door and Mr. Staton handed me candy for by treat bag. The year after Poppa died, in February of 1968, we received a shocking phone call from Nanny. The Statons had been murdered. Both of them.

As my brother and I recalled that fateful day in February, we remembered going down to Nanny's house and her telling us in person the news of the murder. The day was cold and cloudy, and we could see the police and ambulance at the home. Plain clothes detectives wandered out by the chicken yard and went inside the chicken house. We watched as their bodies were loaded and removed. The newspaper gave some of the details the next day and for a while we heard rumors at school that a kid, we knew in our neighborhood was being questioned. Then...it kind of just went away. Nothing. So, I tried the find the news articles or some reports online but came up empty. I thought this was odd but chalked it up to my poor skills to research some things.

I reached out to Jim Sears. Jim is a great guy I went to high school with and reconnected via Facebook over ten years prior. Jim came to be a friend to my family as he helped one of my sons find hard to discover facts regarding a DeMolay project. Jim agreed to try and help. He did not disappoint. Mr. Sears posts articles from the past on a Facebook group page that tracks Denison's history. He always surprises the members by what he is able to find and reveal about our shared hometown. Jim is also to go-to person when questions arise from cloudy memories due to age or wrong information.

This article is one he found in The Bonham Daily Favorite, dated February 14, 1968. The bold headline read: (they mis spelled Denison Police Chief Paul Borum's name several times)

In Denison ...**Parents of Ector Woman Killed**

Mr. and Mrs. W.J. Staton of Denison, parents of Mrs. S.C. Nelms of Ector, were found beaten to death in their home in Denison late Tuesday afternoon by neighbors who went to investigate after they had seen no smoke coming from their chimney or any other activity during the day.

The body of Mrs. Staton, 85, was found on the bed and the body of Mr. Staton was found at the rear of the home in a chicken house. Denison Chief of Police Paul Borom said that a suspect had been arrested and the weapon used in beating Mr. Staton had been found. Chief Borom said that an old piece of flooring with roofing nails driven into it had been used to beat Mrs. Staton about the head and face. The wounds on Mrs. Staton matched the nail heads in the board. The suspected murder weapon was found in a pile of wood under the stove which was used to heat the home. Mrs. Staton was a semi-invalid and used a crutch in walking.

Mr. Staton also had been beaten around the head and had on his shoes and hat when found. He apparently had just slipped on his shoes as they were not tied. Neighbors went to the Staton home later Tuesday afternoon to investigate after seeing no activity around the home during the day. The first neighbor was unable to rouse anyone and called another neighbor and they both went to the Staton home and found the door open. They saw Mrs. Staton's bloody body on the bed and called police, who found Mr. Staton's body at the rear of the home.

Chief Borom said no motive for the slayings had been established Wednesday morning. He said that Texas Ranger Lewis Rigler had been called in to help in the investigation and that the laboratory of the Texas Department of Public Safety would be used in checking the evidence in the case. He said the couple had been dead some 24 hours.

Mr. Staton was born in Fanin County August 19, 1881, son of the late Mr. and Mrs. H.K. Staton. Mrs. Staton, the former Shelby Hayes was born in Farmersville Jan. 1, 1883. They were married at Leonard in 1898 and moved from Trenton to Denison 39 years ago. Funeral services will be held Thursday, at the Bratcher Funeral

Home at 2pm with the Reverend W.D. Emberlin, United Pentecostal Church minister officiating. Interment will be at Carson Cemetery, north of Ector. The couple is survived by a daughter, Mrs. S.C. Nelms of Ector, two sons, Roy A. Staton of Denison and Woodie Staton of Antlers, Okla., 13 grandchildren, and 19 great grandchildren. Mr. Staton had two sisters, Mrs. Florence Sellers of Colbert, Okla., and Mrs. Essie Neely of Whitesboro.

Jim Sears found only one other news article and it concerns the sole suspect in this horrific murder. Once again it was found in the archives of the Bonham newspaper. I can only guess why a Denison murder made the papers in Bonham, and it probably relates to their daughter living in nearby Ector.

The date is Sunday, Feb. 25, 1968, on page 8:

Murder Suspect is Given Test

Denison, Tex. (UPI) – Police said today a suspect in the beating death of Mr. and Mrs. W.T. Staton was given a lie detector test in Dallas Friday. The bodies of the Statons, both in their eighties, were found at their home Feb. 13. Both had been beaten with a floorboard with a nail in it. Police said there were other suspects, and they were being processed. The results of Friday's lie detector test were not yet available, police said.

And that was that. We couldn't find any other articles about this tragic killing that occurred only a few dozen yards away from where our grandmother slept. For the rest of our lives, we have wondered and speculated about the "whys?" and the "who?" of these murders. Is it an unsolved murder case? What went on with the "other suspects" and the lie detector test?

There was another murder a few years later that affected most of us who lived in the Cotton Mill area. Fred Wright was a fixture for us at his grocery store at the corner of Myrick and Florence. When we attended Golden Rule School, it was a delight to walk down to his store for lunch. Hamburgers and Frito chili pies were the favorite for most of us who got to skip the cafeteria sometimes. High school was just up the block, and we would still frequent his store to avoid the lunchroom at school. Lines would form and he would be doing some of the cooking and all of the ringing up the cash register. "Wooly Bully" could be heard from his radio behind the counter. His store was like others before the convenience store concept caught fire. At Fred's you could buy almost anything from milk, bread, eggs, beer, soda pop and magazines, to cooked food he had on special that day. As a paper boy I stopped regularly to buy a cold Dr. Pepper and look for Pepsi bottle caps to redeem at the Rialto Theater on Saturday. Six Pepsi caps got you a free movie when we were kids. No need for mom or dad to take you. We rode our bikes downtown and left them unlocked beside the front of the movie house. Fred Wright was part of the heart and soul of our Cotton Mill life and existence.

Once again, thanks to Jim Sears for this and many more articles about this terrible crime.

Fort Worth Star Telegram May 27, 1970 – page 2

2 Suspects Arrested In Denison Slaying

Denison – Swift action of law enforcement officers in Texas and Oklahoma paid off in the arrest Tuesday of two suspects in the fatal shooting of Charles F. Wright, 44. Wright was found dying in front of his South Denison store by a neighbor who heard two shots shortly before midnight Monday. He had been shot twice in the side with a small caliber pistol. He was pronounced dead on arrival minutes later at a Denison hospital.

The suspects, James Roger Farris,22, and Michael Allen Jewell, 23, were arrested in a motel room at Calera, Okla., north of Denison, by Bryan County Deputy Joe Brimage and were charged with murder with malice and armed robbery before Peace Justice A.L. McGuire at Sherman.

Bryan County officers were waiting delivery of warrants by Texas authorities before arraigning the pair and determining whether or not they would waive extradition to return to Grayson County. Brimage said both men were armed when arrested but offered no resistance. Brimage turned over a 25-caliber pistol taken from the men to Denison Detective Clyde Nave.

Little is known about the suspects except both have records and Jewell has been in and out of Denison for some time. Denison police have a record of half a dozen arrests on him, including burglary. Brimage said the two men were being held on a Federal warrant out of

Kentucky but noted they would be released to Denison on the murder warrant. About $300 was missing from the store's receipts for the day, and a large sum of money was found on the suspects. A neighbor, Kenneth Reeves, said he heard the shots and rushed across the street to the store to find Wright dying on the pavement.

"He didn't say too much," Reeves said, "I asked him if knew who did it and all he could say was he had never seen them before. He was almost dead then and I couldn't understand anything else."

He was a native of Denison and a veteran of World War II. In addition to his wife, he is survived by two sons, Terry and Bill Wright of Denison; his mother, Mrs. Fred Wright of Denison, and a brother, Bob Wright of Denison. Funeral will be at Bratcher Funeral Home here at 10:30 a.m., with burial at Cedarlawn Cemetery.

The story doesn't end here with these duo of murdering robbers. Texas held a trial and found both men guilty and sentenced them to death for their crimes. Farris and Jewell turned out to be some pretty lucky scumbags. While they sat on death row, awaiting appeals, the death penalty was halted by the Supreme Court and their sentences were changed to prison sentences, eligible for parole. A few years later, the death penalty was back on the books, but their parole possibilities remained. Both men were released from prison in the mid-eighties. Jewell went back to Louisville and for all I know is living there today. Farris continued to commit crimes and looks to be free and on parole again.

THE LAST WORD

Remembering Poppa

In the fall of 2020, David and I completed recording the last of our stories about Poppa. In the spring of 2021, I was in the middle of writing these stories. I wondered what was there about Tom Hancock that made him a constant, compelling person in our lives all these years later? The more I pondered this the less convinced I was we could articulate the man in a way anyone else could understand. We talked about this at length and here goes our reasons Poppa was worth having a book about him.

David: "He was from a different time period, 1888. I connected with him and his ideals so much, I felt I was from 1888 also. He moved in a very cool way of life. I clung to him and Nanny. I spent many nights there at their house. If I could be there now, I would."

He's right. We felt a kinship to them we never felt with any of our blood relatives. I wake up some mornings and see David and I sitting on the roof of the little house, under the shade of the pear tree whittling and talking. We could see the lush green gardens from that vantage point. The chickens being fed by Nanny and Poppa walking among his beehives smoking a freshly rolled Bull Durham.

David: "It was three months of not wearing shoes, working in the garden and gathering our lunch straight from the vines. Poppa was full of stories and never let us go hungry. They were special and we knew they loved us. They were not lovey dovey people who hugged and kissed us, but we knew they loved us to the point that defined love."

Poppa wanted to talk to me one time by the carport. Something was bothering him. His father, being a minister, raised him to read and know the Bible. There was a story in Genesis that troubled him, he told me. It is found in Genesis 22.

Sometime later God tested Abraham. He said to him, "Abraham!" "'Here I am, "He replied. Then God said, "Take your son, your only son, whom you love-Isaac- and go to the region of Moriah. Sacrifice him there as a burnt offering on a mountain I will show you."

Early the next morning Abraham got up and loaded his donkey. He took with him two of his servants and his son Isaac. When he had cut enough wood for the burnt offering, he set out for the place God had told him about. On the third day Abraham looked up and saw the place in the distance. He said to his servants, "Stay here with the donkey while I and the boy go over there. We will worship and then come back to you."

Abraham took the wood for the burnt offering and placed it on his son Isaac, and he himself carried the fire and the knife. As the two of them went on together, Isaac spoke up and said to his father Abraham, "Father?"

"Yes, my son?" Abraham replied.

"The fire and the wood are here, "Isaac said, "But where is the lamb for the offering?"

Abraham answered, "God himself will provide the lamb for the burnt offering, my son."

When they reached the place, God had told him about, Abraham built an altar there and arranged the wood on it. He bound his son and laid him on the altar, on top of the wood. Then he reached out his hand and took the knife to slay his son. But the angel of the Lord called out to him from heaven, "Abraham!"

"Here I am," he replied.

"Do not lay a hand on the boy," he said, "Do not do anything to him. Now, I know that you fear God, because you have not withheld from me your son, your only son."

Abraham looked up and there in the thicket he saw a ram caught by his horns. He went over and took the ram and sacrificed it as a burnt offering instead of his son. So, Abraham called that place The Lord Will Provide. And this day it is said, "On the mountain of the Lord it will be provided."

The angel of the Lord called to Abraham a second time and said "I swear by myself, declares the Lord, that because you have done this and have not withheld your son, your only son, I will surely bless you and make your descendants as numerous as the stars in the sky and as the sand on the seashore. Your descendants will take possession of the cities of their enemies and through your offspring all nations on earth will be blessed, because you obeyed me."

As Poppa recounted his story to me in the shade of the old car port at 901 West Dubois, his eyes glistened, and his hands trembled slightly. Poppa was raised to fear God, respect God, to love God. God was in his daily speech and thoughts. Although, I never once saw him visit a church. Ever.

"I don't think I could do that, lay you on an altar and think God wanted me to kill you or harm a hair on your head. I'm afraid I would have to disobey God, whatever judgement would fall on me."

Now, as a child, I had no idea what he was trying to convey to me, other that he loved me. When I got older, I realized that was exactly what he meant. He loved us, all of us.

Television in Denison, Texas, in the 1950's and 60's was a very inexact science back then. Before cable and wifi, there was an antenna. It was a tall pole with metal branches at the top that pointed in several directions. The sets were nearly all black and white and the reception was sometimes poor or nonexistent. The tall antenna was usually taller that the house and when the wind blew, well, it didn't work very well. There was a lot of adjusting when reception was terrible. Channel 12 was our local station and was the easiest to watch. Poppa liked several shows, and one he and Nanny both watched was The Real McCoys, starring Walter Brennan. It told of a family from Appalachia who inherit a farm in the San Fernando Valley in California. Grandpa Amos McCoy, his grandson Luke and wife, Kate, with Little Luke and Hassie, join in with Pepino (the farm's foreman) to start a new life on this farm. Brennan's role as Amos was someone they could identify with in his language, clothing and ideas. While the show was still on the air, I was surprised one day to hear Walter Brennan on the radio performing a song titled "Old Rivers." He didn't actually sing it but narrated a story in his halting familiar voice. It told of a man recalling a childhood friendship with an old farmer. He tells of the man's life as it was full of hard work and hours on end of plowing behind a mule named Midnight. The sun would get high, and that mule would work, and Old Rivers would yell "Whoa!" He would stop and wipe his brow, lean back on the reins and say, "One of these days, I'm gonna climb that mountain, walk up there among them clouds, where the cotton's high, and the corn's a-growing, and there ain't no fields to plow." He ended the song by adding "With the sun beating down across the field, I see that mule, Old Rivers, and me." I always think of Poppa when I hear it. His birth was not remarkable, nor was his death. But his life was very remarkable.

www.ingramcontent.com/pod-product-compliance
Lightning Source LLC
Chambersburg PA
CBHW031630040426
42452CB00007B/765